ULSTER
RICH & RARE

TEXT AND PHOTOGRAPHS BY
Kenneth McNally

 Ulster Television

© Kenneth McNally 1980
Printed by Century Services, Belfast
for the publishers Ulster Television Ltd,
Havelock House, Ormeau Road, Belfast BT7 1EB

ISBN 0 903152 13 4

Contents

The Shape of the Land

If there were such a thing as the typical Ulster scene, it would have to be a composite of many separate images. The landscape of Ulster is rich in physical contrasts, and no one view could be said to be wholly representative. It derives much of its individuality and interest from the variety, both in age and character, of the underlying rocks which give shape and hue to the countryside and produce the marvellously heterogeneous landforms that make travelling through the province such a rewarding experience for the visitor and native Ulsterman alike.

Yet, if the landscape means many things to many people, it is nevertheless possible to look at a particular scene and immediately recognise in it something of the personality of Ulster. There could be no mistaking the gentle ripple of hills which give the green countryside of Co. Down its familiar 'basket of eggs' appearance. During the Ice Age, boulder clay was moulded into *drumlins* — an Irish word, now a recognised geological term, meaning a small ridge. These little ovoid hills occur as swarms of many thousands and extend across the midlands as far as Sligo and Donegal bay in the west. They stand out very clearly along the western side of Strangford Lough and spill over into the lough itself, there forming hump-back islands resembling stranded whales.

Drumlins again appear as islands in Lough Erne where they contribute much to the recreational appeal of the Ulster Lakeland. Here the rocks of the district are Carboniferous limestones which rise to the west of the lakes in bold escarpments, in places riddled with caves and labyrinthine passages which descend far underground to the delight of questing spelaeologists.

But it is the highland and coastal scenery of Ulster which has most evoked the admiration of visitors and carried the name of the province far afield in poetry and song. The breathtaking upsweep of granite which forms the many-peaked Mountains of Mourne at the edge of the Irish Sea is one of the splendours of Co. Down, though sun-seeking holiday-makers on Newcastle beach may have occasion enough to view their cloud-capped summits with apprehension, for the area is one of relatively high rainfall: if you can see the mountains, runs the saying, it is going to rain; if you can't, it is raining already. Disused quarries recall the export trade in granite setts and are a reminder that 'Mourne paved Lancashire'.

Granite appears again in Co. Donegal where it forms the rugged coastal lowlands of the Rosses, outcropping over an area of comparable size to the Mournes. But much harder rocks than granite are responsible for the unkempt grandeur of the Donegal highlands, whose wild and windy acres are so well expressed in the stark outline of Errigle. No purple-headed mountain this, but a bare, silvery-grey mass of scree-mantled quartzite highly resistant to weathering.

Less durable rocks make for less dramatic highland scenery. Though the Sperrins in Co. Tyrone attain heights in excess of 2,000 feet, the softer schists of which they are composed have been worn down more evenly, resulting in mountains which seem subdued by comparison. But if the scenery here sometimes lacks variety it has adequate compensation in the singular beauty of the Glenelly river valley and in the wealth of prehistoric remains recorded from the Sperrins region generally.

Successive outpourings of molten lava in the Tertiary period built up thick layers over much of the province. Though greatly reduced by erosion, the solidified lavas still cover a large area in the north-east where they form the Antrim plateau whose peat-blanketed uplands stretch for mile upon empty mile. Farther south the basalt has warped, creating the wide shallow basin which cradles Lough Neagh, whose waters lap the shores of five counties and drain to the sea via the river Bann. In the west the basalt reaches into Co. Derry, where it rises to 1,260 feet in the frowning escarpments of Binevenagh behind Lough Foyle. Slemish mountain in mid-Antrim is an old volcanic neck looming over the fertile Braid valley, with a chequerboard of stone-walled fields fanning out from its base.

The coastline, too, is rich in rewarding contrasts. Sand-edged bays, abrupt headlands, inaccessible coves and marine caves typify a seaboard of ever-changing moods. In the extreme west the great precipice of Slieve League plunges 1,972 feet to the Atlantic. Alternating basalt and chalk in the north results in a cliff-line of unique character; and basalt also accounts for the striking rock formations of the much-visited Giant's Causeway. This area is instructive about the way in which molten lavas formed a plateau of separate layers, cooling as the familiar hexagonal columns around which an imaginative folklore has grown up. Giants apart, other extravagant theories as to their origin have been put forward from time to time, including one learned dissertation which set out to prove that the columns were the petrified remains of a primeval forest of enormous bamboo.

Modern man has ably exploited the natural features of the coast to enrich the environment, both for his own avocation and for the benefit of tourists. A prehistoric raised beach made possible the construction of the Antrim Coast Road which owes much of its rugged fascination to the aesthetic eye of Charles Lanyon. The craggy cliffs which rise above it are now beyond the reach of the sea except in storms; but are subject to severe erosion by winter rains and frost, with the result that landslips and rockfalls are a frequent occurrence. Along this stretch of coast the abrupt edge of the plateau is cut into by the lovely valleys of the Glens of Antrim.

The attraction of the seacoast is enhanced by a scattering of offshore islands. Most are small, some little more than bare rocky platforms like the Maidens, site of an important lighthouse in the busy shipping lanes of the North Channel; and the Skerries, a chain of wave-washed islets doing useful service as a breakwater for the holiday beaches of Portrush. Several Co. Donegal islands are still inhabited; as is also Rathlin off north Antrim, with a population of about 100, separated from the mainland by the tide-ripped Straits of Moyle. The Copeland Islands, lying at the mouth of Belfast Lough, have only recently been abandoned by their small community.

A distinctive and very Irish feature of the landscape is the capacious peat bog which smothers the surface in a springy carpet of decayed vegetation, its brown monotones relieved by brightly coloured grasses and heathers in season. Blanket bog has been forming continuously since a marked change in climate took place in the first millennium B.C., and for hundreds of years peat, or turf, has been assiduously exploited as a source of domestic fuel by country people. The peat bogs have served another fortuitous purpose, preserving ancient treasures such as gold ornaments and some normally perishable articles, enabling archaeologists and historians to piece together a picture of life in early times. Even large structures were sometimes overwhelmed by the accumulating peat: the great burial tombs of the Stone Age were themselves entombed, to be exposed by turf-cutters two thousand years later. These 'giants' graves' are the first cryptic links in a chain of field monuments tracing man's abiding imprint on the landscape, and we shall return to them in another section.

Church Bay, Rathlin Island, Co. Antrim

The East Maidens lighthouse rock in the North Channel

The Causeway Coast, from seaward

*Columnar basalt formations of
the Giant's Causeway*

Twelve

Castlerock beach, Co. Derry

Chalk cliffs at Kenbane Head, Co. Antrim

The quartzite cliffs of Slieve League, Co. Donegal

Co. Down landscape from the air

Fourteen

The scree-mantled cone of Errigle mountain

Sixteen

The granite peaks of the Mourne Mountains

Slemish mountain, a prominent dolerite hill in the Braid valley

Cave entrances in limestone escarpment, Co. Fermanagh

Glenariff waterfall

Eighteen

The Obscure Past

For thousands of years man has been engaged in moulding the landscape to his particular needs and such has been the extent of his industry that there are few parts of the country, however remote, which do not show some signs of human activity. Hillsides corrugated with old spade ridges reflect an agricultural tradition of great antiquity; today's farmer ploughs land that was first tilled by Neolithic colonists over 5,000 years ago.

Scattered throughout the countryside are countless legacies of Ulster's pioneer farmers. These settlers arrived here around 3500 B.C. and quickly eclipsed the less progressive Mesolithic inhabitants who lived by food-gathering, fishing and hunting. Little evidence of Mesolithic culture survives apart from campsites indicated by refuse heaps called kitchen-middens, and deposits of flint tools; and it is to the ensuing New Stone Age that we must turn to discover the earliest true monuments of the obscure past.

Occupation by Neolithic man is represented by the great chambered tombs in which these people buried their dead. Often spectacular, they belong to the megalithic phase of prehistory and take the form of gallery graves known as court cairns (Ulster horned cairns) and passage graves, the latter often incorporating decorated stones as at Knockmany in Co. Tyrone. Another class of tomb, especially numerous in the northern half of the country, is the portal dolmen. Distinguished by their striking appearance, they impress even the casual observer by their sheer size and pleasing shapes. The term dolmen is derived from a Breton word signifying a stone table. However, they were not used by the druids as altars, nor were they giants' graves as popular folklore would have us believe; but rather they were the sepulchres of important persons whose prestige in life warranted lasting recognition in death. One type in particular, the so-called 'tripod dolmen', exemplified by dramatic Legananny in Co. Down, shows that early man was capable of utilising natural stone to great aesthetic effect.

Many of these structures were originally mounded-over by a cairn of small boulders or earth, which has in the majority of cases been eroded or stripped away for more prosaic uses over the years, leaving the massive orthostats and capstone of the chamber standing in bold isolation. Their immense weight has doubtless been the saving of many from total destruction, and more recently a number have come under State care as National Monuments. But superstition has also played a part in their preservation: country people have in the past as now held them in respect and have been reluctant to remove them from their land. Because of this it is not unusual to see a megalithic tomb in the middle of a field, completely surrounded by crops — Slidderyford, near Newcastle, is a case in point. Others turn up in all kinds of strange places: one stands, improbably, at the front door of a house on the Islandmagee peninsula, Co. Antrim. Another by the roadside near Coagh in Co. Tyrone is partially concealed by a tall hedge which has grown up around it, and its ample capstone is daubed with religious slogans; it has long been subjected to indignities of the sort: a photograph taken in 1914 shows it defaced with auctioneers' posters.

A different kind of monument, less conspicuous than the relics of the ancient tomb-builders but occurring in great number, is the standing stone, sometimes called a *gallaun* or *menhir*. Its purpose is varied. Some are memorials erected over a burial where there is no surface indication of interment; others seem to be boundary markers and a fair number were probably cult objects. Few have been thoroughly investigated.

More interesting but less easily explained are ritual monuments like the magnificent stone circle at Ballynoe in Co. Down, and the curious arrangement of peat-engulfed rings and alignments uncovered at Beaghmore in Co. Tyrone. The site, which came to light in the course of turfcutting in the 1940s, comprises seven circles and a number of associated alignments and cairns, all now isolated in an area of cutaway bog in the bleak moorland to the south of the Sperrin mountains. An early Bronze Age date has been established for this intriguing group of monuments.

The purpose of stone circles has long been debated and they have been interpreted variously as centres of sun-worship, astronomical observatories and druidic temples where human sacrifice was practised. If they were any of these things we are unlikely ever to know, for they remain the most singularly enigmatic of all prehistoric monuments. The few stone circles that have been excavated have been unrewarding in finds and this suggests that they were essentially ritual structures, rather than places of habitation.

The same can be said of that remarkable landmark on the outskirts of Belfast, the Giant's Ring, a huge circular earthwork related to the henge rings, the largest of its kind in Ireland. It encloses a megalithic chamber with passage-grave affinities. Almost certainly this was a ceremonial centre of some considerable importance in the late Neolithic or early Bronze Age.

The arrival of Celtic invaders around 500 B.C. introduced a new item to the landscape which was soon to become widespread. This was the ring-fort settlement, known as a *rath,* consisting of an earth-walled enclosure inside which stood the huts of the occupants. These remains stand out most clearly when seen from the air, such a viewpoint enabling them to be studied in association with their surroundings. Ring-forts were in the main domestic sites serving a pastoral economy, though some of the more elaborate examples probably fulfilled a military function. They sometimes occur in close proximity, as in the neighbourhood of Scarva in Co. Down. In rocky districts stone-built cashels afforded a greater measure of security: the Grianan Aileach in Co. Donegal is one of the finest in the country, complete with (reconstructed) wall terraces and stairways. Surrounding it are the slight remains of three concentric earthworks. Drumena cashel, a large oval ring-fort at Lough Islandreavy, has an extensive souterrain or underground passage in its interior; this has been restored and made accessible to the curious.

As well as the vernacular raths there are some very large earthworks encompassing many acres of a hill-top. A mile or so to the west of Armagh is the royal site of Navan fort, celebrated in ancient legend as the residence of the kings of Ulster in the Celtic Iron Age. Tradition puts the main period of occupation between 300 B.C. and A.D. 332, which accords with archaeological evidence. The fort crowns a drumlin and consists of a circular bank, now heavily tree-grown, with a fosse on the inside. Two mounds in the enclosure have been the subject of recent excavation.

One other type of early homestead calls for mention: the lake-dwelling or *crannog,* the decayed remains of which are numerous though not always recognisable. A true crannog was an artificial island constructed with logs, stones, brushwood, peat and various other materials; but natural lake-islands were also adopted as sites. At Lough na Cranagh on Fair Head is a well preserved walled-island which was probably occupied until a late period.

Slidderyford dolmen, Co. Down, a Neolithic tomb of c2000 B.C.

Kilclooney More dolmen, Co. Donegal

Legananny dolmen in the Slieve Croob hills

Megalithic chamber in the Giant's Ring, Ballynahatty

The Giant's Ring: one of the entrance gaps in the earthwork

Alignments and stone circles at Beaghmore, Co. Tyrone

Ballynoe stone circle, near Downpatrick

Twenty-nine

Lough na Cranagh, a lake-dwelling at Fair Head

Tree-grown earthen rath beside modern farm buildings

Grianan Aileach, a stone cashel 5 miles west-north-west of Londonderry

Thirty-two

Monastery and Castle

The buildings of the early Celtic church were, like the habitations of the Celtic society from which it grew, simple structures of wood and mud, roofed with thatch or shingles and surrounded by ring-walls in the manner of the secular raths. Hardly surprisingly, all the earliest churches have long since disappeared and the oldest surviving examples date from a time when Christianity was already well established in Ireland. Pre-twelfth century churches are recognised by such features as flat-headed (trabeate) doorways with inclined jambs, and pilaster-like projections of the side walls beyond the line of the gables, called antae. The small ruined church at St. John's Point, two miles south of Killough, is representative of the type.

Nendrum on the shores of Strangford Lough gives us a good idea of what an early Celtic monastery must have looked like in its day. Parts of the three concentric cashel walls survive, the innermost being fairly well preserved. Within this enclosure is the church, of which the lower coursings of the side walls and the west gable are standing; a number of cross-slabs found on the site have been inserted into its restored fabric. Near the church is the stump of a round tower. Between the first and second ring-walls are foundations of stone buildings, probably the monks' cells.

The classic hallmark of the Irish monastic scene was the round tower, a tall tapered structure which served as a belfry and as a place of refuge in times of attack. Round towers were built between the tenth and twelfth centuries. Comparatively few are intact today, but the fine example at Antrim rises to 92 feet and still has its conical cap. Of the monastery to which it belonged, however, not a fragment survives. Another complete tower is the well known landmark on Devenish in Co. Fermanagh, notable for some good carved details on the cornice.

More or less contemporary with the round towers and equally symbolic of the Irish monastic tradition, are the high crosses found at a number of sites. Many, like the superb example at Arboe beside Lough Neagh, are richly carved with scriptural themes and intricate interlace designs. There is a somewhat similar one not far away at Donaghmore, also in Co. Tyrone, while a less elaborate high cross is to be found in the Co. Armagh village of Tynan.

The twelfth century saw the appearance of the Romanesque style in church building, characterised by round-headed windows and doorways, at first quite plain but later embellished with profuse ornament based on designs gleaned from the great churches of Europe; but adapted in such a way as to establish Irish Romanesque as a clearly identifiable and uniquely native architectural achievement. Unfortunately little of this *genre* survives in Ulster; but the beautiful Romanesque doorway on the little White Island church in Lower Lough Erne is well worth seeking out.

This same period also witnessed the demise of a great many of the Celtic monasteries as a result of important reforms imposed on the Irish church by St. Malachy of Armagh. From this time onwards, a number of continental monastic Orders were introduced into the country and many existing establishments adopted the new rule. Soon the great medieval abbeys and friaries arose, their noble buildings impressively grand by Irish standards, contributing a more organised appearance to the ecclesiastical architecture of the still predominantly rural landscape. The reform movement sweeping the Irish church was well under way when that other momentous event of the twelfth century, the Anglo-Norman invasion, took place. The invaders also encouraged the influx of continental Orders. Today, even in ruins, Cistercian houses like Grey Abbey on the Ards peninsula and Inch near Downpatrick, both founded under Anglo-Norman patronage, still convey something of their onetime magnificence.

But the most expressive reminder of the Anglo-Norman invasion is found in the great military castles which they built to secure their territorial gains. Before this time true castles were unknown in Ireland, and it may seem strange that what was then an alien feature in the landscape has now become such an accepted part of the Irish scene. The earliest fortifications erected by the Anglo-Normans were wooden towers set atop an earthen mound or 'motte', of which there are numerous examples, including an imposing site at Dromore. When the earth of the motte had become sufficiently compacted to bear the weight of a heavier structure, the wooden towers were replaced by mortared stone buildings. A motte and bailey with fragmentary remains of its castle stands in the village of Clough, Co. Down.

It is, however, the massive stone keeps surrounded by battlemented curtain walls which are most illustrative of the military genius of the Anglo-Normans. As they consolidated their hold on the country, great castles like much-pictured Carrickfergus, lofty Dundrum, and the

Earl of Ulster's fortress at Greencastle in Co. Donegal, dominated the countryside. To the people of the surrounding districts they must have appeared awesome indeed.

The choice of a defensible position was important. Baleful Dunluce, poised uneasily on its storm-battered cliff, occupies the site of an earlier promontory fort, as its prefix *dun* indicates. A former residence of the MacDonnells, it was abandoned in the latter part of the seventeenth century. The precarious nature of the site had been fearfully demonstrated in 1639 when the entire domestic wing collapsed into the sea with much loss of life. The ruins form a very striking object, especially at dusk when its shattered towers and gables are silhouetted against the western sky.

Not all castles were so grand. In the fifteenth and sixteenth centuries many lesser fortifications, aptly called tower houses, were built by chieftains and landowners to provide protection for themselves and their retainers. Narrow Water castle at the neck of Carlingford Lough is a picturesque and well preserved late example. It has the usual defensive features found in a building of this type: machicolation, loop windows and murder hole; the enclosing bawn has been rebuilt.

Very characteristic of Ulster are the seventeenth-century plantation castles erected by grantees of confiscated lands. These buildings form a distinct class and often have architectural traits derived from Scottish styles, notably the round corner turrets so well displayed on Ballygally castle, Co. Antrim. The Scottish influence is again seen in that rather remarkable building, Monea castle in Co. Fermanagh, built by Malcolm Hamilton in 1618. Its most distinctive feature is the entrance with its flanking circular towers from which sprout square chambers, diagonally aligned on the towers and united to them by crow-stepped gables.

About the same time, Sir Basil Brooke was adapting the O'Donnell castle in Donegal town to a similar purpose. Among the general improvements he made was the insertion of an ornate Jacobean fireplace, richly decorated with coats of arms and other devices. Alongside the great tower, he built a very beautiful gabled manor house with large mullioned windows. The requirements of defence were slowly being relaxed in favour of elegance and comfort; and if peaceful times were not exactly round the corner, the era of the castle was nevertheless coming to an end.

Arboe high cross, Co. Tyrone

Nendrum monastery, Mahee Island, Strangford

Thirty-eight

White Island, Lower Lough Erne:
figure sculpture and Romanesque doorway

Devenish monastery, Co. Fermanagh

Forty

Inch Abbey, a twelfth-century Cistercian monastery

Tynan high cross, Co. Armagh

Carrickfergus Castle: eloquent symbol of Anglo-Norman power in Ulster

Narrow Water castle, a sixteenth-century tower house with enclosing bawn

Dundrum castle, a twelfth-century Anglo-Norman castle with cylindrical keep

The entrance façade of Massereene Castle
in Antrim town; the ruins have been demolished

*Fireplace inserted in Donegal castle
by Sir Basil Brooke in the
early seventeenth century*

Monea castle, Co. Fermanagh: a fine example of a plantation castle built in the Scottish style

Dunluce castle, a rock-bound fortress on the north coast, onetime residence of the MacDonnells

Town and Country

The traditional Ulster farm with its solid stone-built house and cluster of outbuildings standing in a walled yard may be likened to the Celtic rath of old. Both share a preference for isolation as self-contained domestic units; and we might see in the stout cylindrical gate-pillars of the former a parallel with the timber posts which once flanked the entrances to the pastoral raths.

Towns did not become a homogeneous item in the Ulster landscape until the seventeenth century. Some few (Carrickfergus, for example) can trace their origins to the Anglo-Norman presence in medieval times; but the majority came into existence during the plantations which followed the flight of the earls in 1607, when Scots and English colonists received grants of confiscated lands from the Crown. Although some of these settlements failed in later years, most expanded and prospered with the coming of industrialisation.

It was the introduction of cotton-spinning in the 1770s which heralded the start of the industrial revolution in Ulster. Linen manufacture in the eighteenth century was essentially a domestic occupation carried on by weavers who were also farmers. Cotton-spinning on the other hand was a factory process from the beginning, employing many female workers and bringing people into the towns from outlying areas. The first steam-powered cotton mill in Ireland was operating in Lisburn in 1789. When the cotton industry faltered in the 1820s, largely as a result of the challenge from Lancashire, an increasing number of the mills switched to linen manufacture.

A great deal of urban rebuilding took place in the eighteenth century and it was then that many Ulster towns acquired their enduring features. The broad, house-lined streets typical of today's townscapes date mostly from this time. Some small industrial centres which arose in the nineteenth century were a direct consequence of the developing linen trade. Sion Mills, the attractive if un-Irish model mill village founded by the Herdman family in 1835 on a site beside the Mourne river in Co. Tyrone, is one such.

Industrialisation and urban growth notwithstanding, Ulster's towns remain thoroughly countrified in spirit: green fields and hills bright with yellow whin press in on all sides. The perpetuity of colourful folk customs like the annual Lammas Fair held in Ballycastle, and many lesser events of the kind, are vivid expressions of deep-rooted pastoral traditions of forgotten antiquity.

The timeless quality of the countryside is heightened by the decaying wreckage of rural industry. Old watermills moulder picuresquely beside streams which once supplied their motive power; derelict barges lie half-submerged in forgotten inland waterways, and disused railway stations stripped of track and invaded by weeds await trains that never arrive.

The working windmill, once a serene part of the Ulster scene, is now a thing of the past. Crumbling shells dotted here and there tell their own story of obsolescence, and only one complete example survives: the restored eighteenth-century tower mill at Ballycopeland near Millisle. For more than a hundred years it remained in the possession of one family, but had been unused since 1915 and is now in State care. The top section is constructed as a revolving turret which allowed the sails to be set into the wind by adjustment of the fantail; this explains the need for two doors, since if the turning sails blocked one entrance the alternative was used. When the whirring sails were in full flight the throb of cog-wheels and gears and the creak of timber shafts was transmitted to the walls, so that the entire mill pulsated with life. Cartloads of corn delivered to the miller were hoisted to the hopper at the top of the mill, through which the grain was dispensed to the millstones on the next level, and thence to the ground floor.

Scenic coastal towns and villages abound. Resort centres like Portrush, Portstewart, Ballycastle and Bangor support a sizeable tourist industry and are convenient bases from which to explore the variegated shoreline with its numerous small harbours, coastal walks, offshore islands and seabird sanctuaries. Timely recognition of the recreational importance of the countryside has resulted in legislation to control development in areas of outstanding natural beauty. Close to Belfast, the opening of the Lagan valley public footpath has provided a valuable amenity; and within a few miles of the city centre the industrial landscape of shipyard and oil refinery gives onto the sailing waters of Co. Down.

The seaport of Londonderry, second city of the North and 'Maiden City' of 1690 fame, preserves its seventeenth-century town walls, which are the most complete in Britain. Outside the boundaries of the old plantation town stands the Gothic-style Guildhall, erected in 1908 and incorporating good stained glass windows depicting episodes from Derry's long and emotive history.

Most of the best town architecture in Ulster belongs to the Georgian era of the eighteenth and early nineteenth century, a time of energetic building activity which produced the elegant limestone houses of Armagh and the very dignified Hillsborough courthouse constructed of Mourne granite and Scrabo sandstone. Founded by the Hills family in the eighteenth century, Hillsborough is one of the most pleasant small towns in the province, its character lately much enhanced by the provision of a by-pass road to reduce the volume of motor traffic in its streets. In the seventeenth century it had been an important military post on the Belfast-Dublin routeway and the star-shaped fort built by Colonel Arthur Hill still stands; the squat tower house with corner turrets in the south-east wall was a later insertion.

Out in the country, palatial houses like Castle Coole in Co. Fermanagh and Mount Stewart in Co. Down, reflected the affluence of the landed aristocracy. It is a paradox that both are now maintained through a charity.

Although perhaps most closely associated in the public mind with the acquisition of great houses, the National Trust is active in preserving good vernacular architecture in Northern Ireland. There are many examples of its enlightened policy: Cushendun village with its handsome Maud cottages in an idyllic setting of river and glen; Coolanlough cottage in Fair Head clachan; and Kearney village, a formerly dilapidated fishing hamlet on the Ards peninsula. Deserted since the Second World War, Kearney was acquired by the Trust in 1965 and after repair the individual sites were leased to private occupiers. Other projects include the refurbishing of Gray's Printing Shop in Strabane where John Dunlap, who later secured a niche in history as the printer of the American Declaration of Independence, served his apprenticeship. A collection of demoded farm equipment forms the basis of an agricultural museum at Ardress House in Co. Armagh; and at Wellbrook in Co. Tyrone an eighteenth-century water-powered beetling mill has been restored to working order.

The conservation of fine buildings is also the concern of the Ulster Architectural Heritage Society, whose compendious surveys have done so much to create an awareness of the architectural wealth of the province; while the excellent Ulster Folk and Transport Museum occupying 180 acres of Co. Down parkland is one of the foremost of its kind in Europe.

Portstewart harbour and promenade, Co. Derry

Fifty-four

Thatched country house in Co. Down

Georgian houses in the Mall, Armagh

Water-powered spade mill, Cultra Folk Museum

Beetling rollers in Wellbrook mill, Co. Tyrone

Central drive-shaft gear system in Ballycopeland windmill

Ballycopeland windmill

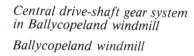

Fifty-six

Fifty-seven

Ballycastle Lammas Fair, 1960

Coolanlough clachan, Co. Antrim

Disused railway station at Saintfield

Ballintoy harbour

Glenelly valley, Co. Tyrone

Trawbreaga bay, Inishowen, Co. Donegal

Sixty-six

Six-mile-water in Massereene demesne, Antrim

Sailing at Cultra, Co. Down

Sion Mills, a nineteenth-century industrial village in Co. Tyrone

Contrasting examples of National Trust properties: left *Castle Coole in Co. Fermanagh;* below *Kearney hamlet in Co. Down*

Country road and farmstead

Seventy

Aerial view of Hillsborough showing fort and church

DERRY IN 1793.

Stained glass windows in the Guildhall, Londonderry

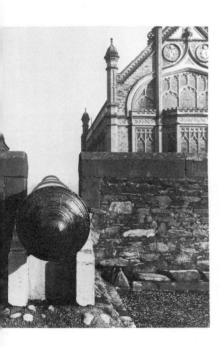

Thatched cottage in Co. Antrim

Seventy-four

Town houses in Lisburn

Gray's Printing Shop, Strabane, Co. Tyrone

A Belfast Vignette

Despite considerable redevelopment which has introduced many new shapes to the city skyline in recent years, Belfast retains much of the character of a progressive nineteenth-century town formed by the industrial revolution. In a century of remarkable expansion, resulting initially from cotton-spinning and later and more importantly from linen production and shipbuilding, Belfast grew from a modest market town of some 20,000 inhabitants in 1800, to a vigorous trading and manufacturing centre with a population of 350,000 by 1900.

Many nineteenth-century visitors to Belfast commented on the healthy spirit of commerce that was everywhere in evidence: 'The men have a business look', observed Thackeray in 1842, and that business look was echoed by reassuringly solid office and warehouse blocks built with an air of permanence. James Adair Pilson, writing four years later, was full of praise for High Street, then the principal thoroughfare. It was 'airy, wide, and of imposing aspect, and makes amends, by the magnificence of its shops and warehouses, and by its clean and cheerful appearance, together with the enlivening excitement caused by a perfect whirl of business, for some irregularity in its alignment and architectural structure.'

Of eighteenth-century public buildings there survives intact the worthy edifice of the Belfast Charitable Society (1771) in North Queen Street. Another important public building of the period still stands in Waring Street, though under such heavy disguise that its original features cannot now be discerned. This, the Belfast Exchange, built in 1769 and provided with second storey Assembly Rooms a few years later, was transformed by Charles Lanyon in 1845 into prestigeous premises for the Belfast Banking Company. The rich Italianate façade wears well and forms an imposing landmark when viewed across the open aspect of Bridge Street.

There are some elegant Georgian houses on the south side of Chichester Street, while earlier in date and more countrified is the late eighteenth-century house tucked away in a courtyard off Garfield Street. Slum clearance schemes have done away with many of the old degenerate housing enclaves close to the city centre. Carrick Hill Place with its picturesque but insanitary cottages is long gone; as is also, with a greater sense of community loss, the old Smithfield Market, beloved of browsers who loitered about its dusty bookshelves, stacks of seventy-eight records and curious bric-a-brac. Smithfield had been the scene of an open air market since about 1780, dealing in livestock and agricultural produce. It was described by John Gough in 1814 as a large square 'laid out for a cattle market, called Smithfield, the centre of which is surrounded by a wooden paling, to confine the cattle, outside of which, at the distance of a moderate street, good brick houses have been erected.' Smithfield acquired more permanent form in the mid-nineteenth century when the familiar quadrangle of single-storey shops and connecting grid of covered passageways was laid out. Its agreeable through-otherness was not without a certain fascination, and the new market, for all its phoenix-like rise from the ashes of the old, seems a lesser place in comparison.

Great changes have also taken place in the entries, that warren of evocative passageways between High Street and Ann Street. From their beginnings as rights of way through the gardens of private houses fronting High Street in the late seventeenth century, the passages were themselves built up with dwellings and merchants' yards. Until quite recently they preserved a pleasing sense of period: wall-mounted gas lamps and signboards, decorative plaster and ironwork, mellowed brick walls, cobbles and setts underfoot.

Commercial and public buildings of the later nineteenth century were often richly ornamented with fine carving. Architectural sculpture flourished in Belfast at this time and many an otherwise staid façade was enlivened with inventive and extrovert designs executed in durable stone. If, like the Victorian parlour song, some of this work appears overtly sentimental and pretentious, it can be appreciated and enjoyed on account of its quality, which is generally high. The sculptures of Thomas Fitzpatrick, seen to good effect on the Custom House and on the McCausland building in Victoria Street, will repay study.

It was not only esteemed buildings that were enriched in this way. The ordinary public house sometimes came in for quite out-of-the-ordinary treatment. The Crown Liquor Saloon in Great Victoria Street is, or rather was (for it has sustained a fair amount of bomb damage) a splendid monument to the late Victorian period. It is a treasure house of exuberant ornament, coloured glass and tiles, marble, oak, and the glint of well-polished brass. The present landlord is the National Trust, who are restoring the building to its original state piecemeal. The moulds for the exterior tiles of the Crown (made by Royal Doulton) have been located in the Ironbridge Museum and are to be used in the manufacture of replacements.

The Elephant House bar in North Street has a pleasantly Raj-ish portal; while that of the Morning Star in Pottinger's Entry is sentinelled by a very sober-looking winged lion. The industrious colleen who tended her spinning wheel above the Ulster House in Ormeau Road was removed during modernisation a decade or more ago. A similar fate befell many another interesting piece of architectural sculpture. Many will remember the attractive arch at the entrance to Wilson's Court in High Street; and, not a hundred yards away, the tactfully symbolic statues on the Scottish Widow's Fund building. Both were demolished in 1961.

There are, however, some colourful survivals. The stupendous but sadly neglected Dunville fountain at the junction of Falls Road and Grosvenor Road is a strange monster to occupy so small a public park — 'presented as a free gift to the city by Robert G. Dunville of Redburn.' Erected in 1891, it is the largest and most elaborate of a number of memorial fountains in the city. To the same year belongs the façade of Belfast Gasworks in Ormeau Road, somewhat resembling the curtain wall of a medieval fortress. So overwhelming is this great wall that one tends to loose sight of the intricacies of its decorative panels, mouldings and friezes. Its south end terminates in a massive brick gable at the top of which is the city coat of arms.

Another building of highly individual character is the Grand Opera House, built in 1895 to designs by the prolific Victorian and Edwardian theatre architect, Frank Matcham. It has lately been scrupulously (and lovingly) refurbished, conserving much of the splendid detailing of the auditorium.

In a city which is also a port, it is not surprising to find frequent reminders of its time-honoured links with the sea. A plaster lifebelt adorns the front of Tedford's Ships Chandlers in Donegall Quay; a stone anchor is featured on the pediment over the entrance to the Ulster Brewery in Sandy Row; strange-looking fish that nature never designed entwine their scaly bodies around the bases of lamp standards (shorn of their lanterns) on the parapets of the old Queen's Bridge. There is an amazing (and one imagines distracting) array of shipboard *memorabilia* in Sinclair Seamen's Presbyterian Church in Corporation Square.

Entrance gateway to Clifton House in North Queen Street

The Belfast Bank (now Northern Bank) in Waring Street, Charles Lanyon's 1840s transformation of the old Belfast Exchange and Assembly Rooms

Victims of 1961 demolition
in High Street:
above *entrance arch of Wilson's Court;*
right *symbolic statues on Scottish*
Widow's Fund building

Carrick Hill Place, now demolished

Eighty-four

Stone sculpture by Thomas Fitzpatrick in Victoria Street

Lamp Standards on Queen's Bridge

Toll house, formerly at corner of Lisburn Road and Bradbury Place

Decorative iron fanlight grilles: above in High Street; below left in Royal Avenue

Dunville Park fountain, Falls Road, erected in 1891

Eighty-seven

Public house decoration:
above right and left *the
Crown Liquor Saloon in Great
Victoria Street;*
below right *the Elephant House
in North Street*

The Morning Star in Pottinger's Entry

Eighty-nine

Ninety

Crown Entry in 1960

Setts in Joy's Entry

*Pottinger's Entry, looking from
High Street end with
Churchill House rising high
in the background*

*Ann Street entrance to
Pottinger's Entry*

Auditorium detail, Grand Opera House

Smithfield Market as it was in the 1960s

Pediment carving on Belfast Gasworks